I Love Sports

Tennis

by Allan Morey

Bullfrog
Books

Ideas for Parents and Teachers

Bullfrog Books let children practice reading informational text at the earliest reading levels. Repetition, familiar words, and photo labels support early readers.

Before Reading

- Discuss the cover photo. What does it tell them?
- Look at the picture glossary together. Read and discuss the words.

Read the Book

- "Walk" through the book and look at the photos. Let the child ask questions. Point out the photo labels.
- Read the book to the child, or have him or her read independently.

After Reading

- Prompt the child to think more. Ask: Have you watched a tennis match? Have you ever hit a tennis ball with a racket? What do you think would be most fun about tennis?

Bullfrog Books are published by Jump!
5357 Penn Avenue South
Minneapolis, MN 55419
www.jumplibrary.com

Library of Congress Cataloging-in-Publication Data

Morey, Allan.
 Tennis / by Allan Morey.
    pages cm. — (I love sports)
Summary: "This photo-illustrated book for early readers introduces the basics of tennis and encourages kids to try it. Includes labeled diagram of tennis court and photo glossary." — Provided by publisher.
 Includes index.
 ISBN 978-1-62031-183-7 (hardcover) —
 ISBN 978-1-62496-270-7 (ebook)
1. Tennis for children—Juvenile literature. I. Title.
GV1001.4.C45H64 2015
796.342—dc23
                                    2014036867

Series Editor: Rebecca Glaser
Series Designer: Ellen Huber
Book Designer: Anna Peterson
Photo Researcher: Jenny Fretland VanVoorst

Photo Credits: All photos by Shutterstock except: Corbis, 6–7, 8, 10–11, 11, 18–19, 20–21, 23tl, 23tr; Dreamstime, 3, 23bl; SuperStock, 12–13, 14–15, 23ml; Thinkstock, 23mr.

Printed in the United States of America at Corporate Graphics in North Mankato, Minnesota.

Table of Contents

Let's Play Tennis!

Grab a ball.

Get your racket.

Let's play!

Sara has the ball.

She serves first.

The ball goes over the net.

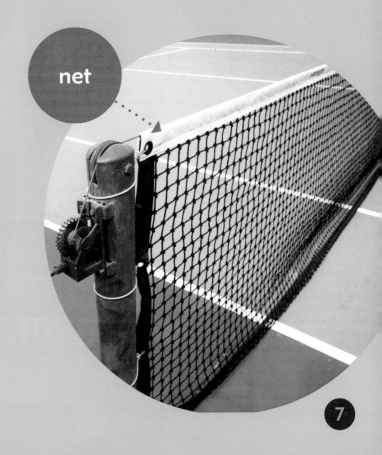

net

Mike hits the ball.

It flies back to Sara.

The players volley.
They take turns hitting
the ball.

It goes back and forth.

Ceon slams the ball over the net.

Tim swings.

He misses.

Ceon scores a point.

Mia hits the ball.

It flies out of bounds.

The other player
gets a point.

out of bounds

Sam hits the ball.

It goes into the net.

The other player gets a point.

Sara scores the last point.
She wins the match!

Do you want to play?

Hit the ball.

Tennis is fun!

At the Tennis Court

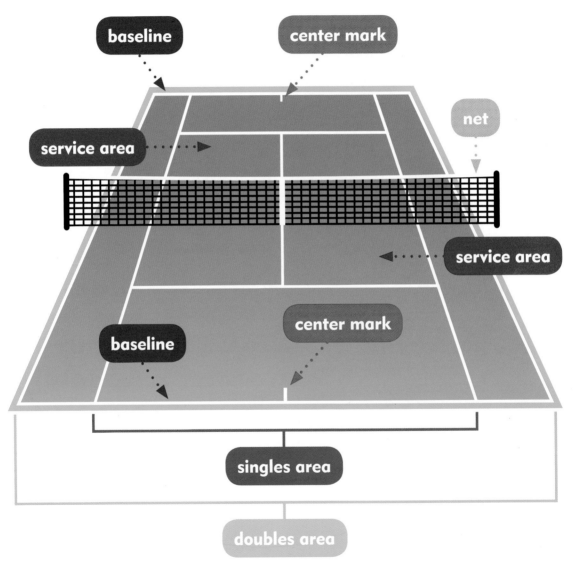

baseline

center mark

net

service area

service area

baseline

center mark

singles area

doubles area

Picture Glossary

match
A game of tennis is called a match; matches are divided into several sets.

serve
To make the first hit of the ball, which starts play; players take turns serving.

out of bounds
A ball is out of bounds if it lands beyond the outer lines on a tennis court.

slam
To hit something with great force, such as using a racket to hit a tennis ball.

racket
A piece of equipment used to hit a tennis ball.

volley
When two people hit the ball back and forth over the net several times.

Index

match 19	score 12, 19
net 7, 12, 16	serve 7
out of bounds 14	slam 12
points 12, 14, 17, 19	turns 11
racket 4	volley 11

To Learn More

Learning more is as easy as 1, 2, 3.

1) Go to www.factsurfer.com

2) Enter "tennis" into the search box.

3) Click the "Surf" button to see a list of websites.

With factsurfer.com, finding more information is just a click away.